AF583823

for Dad, Mum & Mel

First published in Australia in 2026 by Thames & Hudson Australia
Wurundjeri Country, 132A Gwynne Street, Cremorne, Victoria 3121

29 28 27 26 5 4 3 2 1

ISBN 978-1-76076-543-9

A catalogue record for this book is available from the National Library of Australia

Designed by Dave Petzold
Typeset in New Century Schoolbook
Printed and bound in China by C&C Offset Printing Co., Ltd

Thames & Hudson Australia wishes to acknowledge that Aboriginal and Torres Strait Islander peoples are the first storytellers of this nation and the Traditional Custodians of the land on which we live and work. We acknowledge their continuing culture and pay respect to Elders past and present.

thamesandhudson.com.au

We Live on a Boat

DAVE PETZOLD

We live on a boat. She's called Lucky Sea Legs.

We call her that because we always tumble into good things.

Lucky Sea Legs has a ladder that goes all the way up and an anchor that goes all the way down.

Kank-kank-kank-kank!

16

This is the galley, where we eat breakfast, and that's Salad, our boat iguana.

Salad loves to sleep on the radio.

Crackle! Hissss!

Every morning
we plan our trip
in the map room
(it's actually the
galley, but don't
tell anyone).

Dad works out how
far we need to go
and I draw our
path on the map.

Scritch! Scratch!

We live on a boat
and every day we
learn new things.

Mum teaches us how
to speak Spanish
and Dad shows us
how to fix the boat.

Sometimes we learn
maths or history,
but learning to surf
is my favourite.

Shakaaaa!

DRUMS UKULELES TAMBOR-INES
BEST PRICE
Cheese

Today, we need supplies, so we take the tender to the mainland.

Dad and Sunny buy pawpaws and apples, and Mum stocks up on spices.

I buy a ukulele.

Twang! Twang!

When it's time to go we all help to get Lucky Sea Legs ready.

Sunny closes all the hatches.

Mum checks the weather station.

Dad pulls up
the anchor.

And I set the jib.
Click-click-click! Whoosh!

Today, it's my turn to steer the boat.
The wind is warm and the clouds have gone somewhere else.

Stingrays fly from the water.
Flip-flap! Flip-flap!

We live on a boat and we like to explore tropical islands and camp on the beach.

We make a fire and watch baby turtles hatch.

Pip! Pop! Chirp!

In the morning we snorkel through a giant kelp forest.
Cuttlefish slide between the rocks.

We watch seals twist and bend as they chase fish.
Swooosh!

We look above us,

below us,

and all around us.

We live on a boat
and we meet lots
of people who live
on boats, too.

After dinner we
tell stories and
play music.

I bang on the
bongo drums.

Bup-bom-bup-bom!

Tonight, the moon is bright
and the coral are spawning.

We dive down and watch thousands
of tiny eggs silently float by.

In the morning the sun is up
early and so are the whales.

Their song echoes through the boat.

Ooowraaaaaeeeeeeeii!

We cast off into the sunrise.

'Where should we sail today?' Dad asks.

'Wherever the wind takes us!' we all shout.

I set the jib.

Click-click-click! Whoosh!